HARLEY AND THE DAVIDSONS

Other Badger Biographies

HARLEY AND THE DAVIDSONS

Motorcycle Legends

PETE BARNES

WISCONSIN HISTORICAL SOCIETY PRESS

Published by the Wisconsin Historical Society Press
Publishers since 1855

© 2007 by State Historical Society of Wisconsin

wisconsin history.org

Photographs identified with PH, WHi, or WHS are from the Society's collections; address inquiries about such photos to the Visual Materials Archivist at the above address.

Use of the images on pages 7, 8 (top), 10, 11, 30, 31, 36, and 40 is courtesy of Herbert Wagner.

Printed in the United States of America
Designed by Jill Bremigan

13 12 11 10 09   2 3 4 5 6

Library of Congress Cataloging-in-Publication Data

Barnes, Pete.
  Harley and the Davidsons : motorcycle legends / by Pete Barnes.
      p. cm.
  Includes bibliographical references and index.
  ISBN-13: 978-0-87020-380-0 (pbk. : alk. paper)
  1. Harley Davidson motorcycle—History—Juvenile literature. 2. Harley-Davidson Incorporated—History—Juvenile literature. 3. Harley family—Juvenile literature. 4. Davidson family—Juvenile literature.
I. Title.
  TL448.H3B36 2008
  338.7'6292275092273—dc22
                          2006026666

Front cover: Illustration courtesy of the Wisconsin Historical Society. Back cover: Photos courtesy of Harley-Davidson.

∞ The paper used in this publication meets the minimum requirements of the American National Standard for Information Sciences—Permanence of Paper for Printed Library Materials, ANSI Z39.48-1992.

Contents

1

Two Friends Share a Dream

Bill Harley and his best friend Arthur Davidson loved to go fishing near their childhood homes in Milwaukee, Wisconsin. They rode their bicycles to and from the lakes, pedaling hard to get home before dark. One day, as they struggled up a hill on their way back from a favorite lake, the boys imagined building motors for their bicycles to make the climb easier.

This is how Milwaukee looked when Bill Harley and Arthur Davidson invented their first motorized bike.

The year was 1891, and they were 10. Little did they know that in just 20 years they would become America's number one motorcycle **manufacturers** (man yoo **fak** chur urs). Or that 100 years later boys and girls around the world would know about the power and speed of Harley-Davidson motorcycles. Arthur and Bill never imagined their idea would make them rich and famous. They just wanted a way to get home from their fishing trips more quickly.

Bill and Arthur didn't invent the motorcycle. They **adapted** other people's ideas and made them better. Like lots of people at the end of the 1800s, they were fascinated by machines and wanted to learn more about them. Both boys were smart and hardworking, but they preferred tinkering with tools in Arthur's basement to doing schoolwork.

Exciting new machines were everywhere near the end of the nineteenth century.

manufacturer: a company that makes something, often using machines
adapted: changed for a particular use or situation

2

The 2 friends were constantly together. Bill was a tall and quiet boy with serious eyes. Arthur was shorter and loved to talk and share ideas. They didn't listen when people told them they were wasting their time. Some of their friends thought they were crazy for spending so much time working in the dark basement instead of playing sports or chasing after girls. To Arthur and Bill, working with machines was just more fun. They kept striving for their dreams, never giving up even when the work was difficult.

Great ideas were changing the world as these boys dreamed. Alexander Graham Bell's telephone had allowed people from different parts of the country to talk to each other. Karl Benz's automobile would soon make it possible to travel more than 100 miles in one day. The light bulb, the dishwasher, and the vacuum cleaner were

An early electric light bulb

other new inventions that were making life easier. Inventions such as these, as well as the factories that made them, were all part of the Industrial Revolution.

The Industrial Revolution

The Industrial Revolution began in England in the late 1700s and quickly spread to North America and other parts of the world. In the late 1800s, the United States experienced rapid change as factories were built and people moved from farm living to industrial jobs in cities. Machines now **produced** many products that had been made by hand. Railroads were built to transport goods across the country. New products made life easier for many Americans. However, the factories often had terrible working conditions and led to overcrowded cities and increased pollution.

WHI IMAGE ID 24556

Building new railroads was difficult and sometimes dangerous work.

produced: made, put together

Milwaukee played a big part in the Industrial Revolution as people moved from farms into cities and used technology to improve their lives. Milwaukee became famous for its **iron foundries**, **breweries** (**broo** ur eez), and meatpacking plants, which hired thousands of workers. Barges carried goods down Lake Michigan toward Chicago, and people heard railroad whistles all over the city.

Arthur's father, William C. Davidson, worked as a carpenter for the Milwaukee Road Railway. Arthur's 2 older brothers, William A. and Walter, also worked in the railroad

Can you believe how many machines fit into this crowded machine shop?

shops building parts and keeping the trains running smoothly. Arthur and Bill often visited the shops. They learned a lot about machines and tools by watching the railroad men as they worked.

iron foundry: a factory that melts and shapes metal   **brewery:** a factory that produces beer

5

The boys also spent a lot of time on their bicycles, like many people at that time in Milwaukee. By 1896 there were around 4 million bicycles in the United States and 250 bicycle companies. Bicycles were inexpensive, easy to operate, and fairly easy to repair.

Bicycles made getting around town easy and fun.

Motorcycles were another story. Bicycles with motors did exist, but in small numbers. Most people considered these motorized bikes mystery machines. Lots of inventors had fiddled with them, but few had succeeded. They found it was tough to build a motor small and light enough to fit a bicycle frame.

SCIENTIFIC AMERICAN

This early French motorcycle looks quite different from the motorcycles we ride today.

How did Arthur and Bill know about motorcycles if so few existed? It is likely that the first motorcycle they ever saw was owned by an inventor named Edward Pennington. Pennington was known for his weird inventions, including a motorized baby buggy and a flying machine sometimes called a "gas boy." Few of his inventions actually worked, but they got a lot of attention because they were so unusual.

In 1895, Pennington brought his motorcycle to Milwaukee for a demonstration. Posters advertised his amazing machine, and people waited excitedly on Grand Avenue for his demonstration to begin. Pennington told reporters his motorcycle could race up to 58 miles per hour. It is doubtful that it could go that fast. But regardless of its speed, it was an exciting sight for the huge crowd.

Do you think the Pennington motorcycle could really fly through the air like this picture claims?

Bill Harley and Arthur Davidson were 14 that summer. They lived just a few blocks from Grand Avenue. The chances are good that they were in the crowd that saw Edward Pennington go whizzing up and down the street. Perhaps Pennington inspired them to think more about building their own motorcycle.

Grand Avenue in Milwaukee where Edward Pennington rode his motorcycle

Lots of people were thinking about motorcycles by 1895. Sylvester Roper had built a bicycle powered by a steam boiler more than 20 years earlier. Imagine having a coal-burning boiler sitting under your seat! Gottlieb Daimler (**Got** leeb **Dime** ler) built the first gasoline-powered bicycle in 1885. His bicycle was made mostly of wood and had small wheels on each side like training wheels on a kid's bike. These early motor-bicycles were clumsy and did not ride well on bumpy roads.

Two Frenchmen named Comte de Dion (**Comb** deh Dee **own**) and his toymaker friend Georges Bouton (**Jorj** Boo **tone**) helped solve this problem with a miniature engine that fit well into a bicycle frame. The De Dion–Bouton engine weighed just 40 pounds and could operate at high speeds for a long period of time. It was made of aluminum and produced ½ **horsepower**. What's amazing is that this basic engine design is still used on most motorcycles more than 100 years later.

Horsepower

The term *horsepower* was created by the engineer James Watt, who lived during the 1700s. He wanted a way to talk about the power available from horses lifting coal from a coal mine. One horsepower is equal to one horse moving 330 pounds of coal 100 feet in one minute. Many machines are measured in horsepower today to show how much work they can accomplish or how fast they can accelerate. Some motorcycles today have 100 horsepower or more.

horsepower: a unit for measuring the power of an engine

The De Dion–Bouton engine inspired American inventors to create motorcycles of their own. Most of these Americans were bicycle manufacturers who built engines to attach to their bicycles. In 1901, an

" The Motor Cycle that made Milwaukee famous. "

An early ad for Merkel motorcycles

explosion of these motor-bicycles rocked the United States. New companies and new brands came from every corner of the country. "Indian" motorcycles rolled out of Springfield, Massachusetts; "Mitchells" came from Racine, Wisconsin; and "Merkel" motorcycles were built in Bill and Arthur's hometown of Milwaukee.

But Bill and Arthur's dream of building a motorcycle would have to wait. Just a year after Edward Pennington's visit to Milwaukee, the Harley family moved to Milwaukee's north side. That same year Arthur Davidson moved to his grandparents' farm in Cambridge, Wisconsin. The 2 childhood friends were no longer in the same neighborhood, but they kept in touch through letters and occasional visits.

That year, Bill began working at a company called Meiselbach. It was a bicycle factory. He helped assemble bicycles and drew designs for new models. Arthur also kept his interest in machines alive. He worked on his grandparents' farm, but he also worked as a **pattern maker** for local companies. A pattern maker uses saws to cut wood and a **lathe** (layth) to shape the

Bill Harley learned a lot about designing machines while working at a bicycle factory similar to this one.

wood into different patterns. These patterns were turned into metal **castings** that could be reproduced again and again. They were used to build all sorts of engine parts, tools, and pieces of machines.

pattern maker: a person who shapes wood to make patterns for machine parts
lathe: a machine in which a piece of wood or metal is held and turned while being shaped by a tool
casting: an object cast or created in a mold

While in Cambridge, Arthur met Ole (**Oh** lee) Evinrude, who also was interested in motorized machines. Arthur and Ole fished together in an old rowboat on Lake Ripley. They took turns with the oars and discussed how nice it would be to have a small motor to save their aching shoulders from all that rowing. Just like Bill and Arthur's idea for a motorized bicycle, Arthur and Ole's idea would one day make Ole Evinrude a very successful businessman. Evinrude Motor Company became one of the largest manufacturers of **outboard motors** for boats in the world.

Back in Milwaukee, Bill Harley missed his old friend Arthur. In 1900 he wrote Arthur and told him there were good jobs for pattern makers in Milwaukee. Arthur moved back to town, and soon both young men were working for an electric motor company called Pawling and Harnischfeger.

Soon after Arthur's return, the 2 friends attended a variety show at the Bijou Theater. They enjoyed all of the singing and dancing performances, but one act near the end made them forget all the rest. A French actress named Anna Held

outboard motor: a motor with a propeller that can be attached to the rear of a small boat

12

rode across the stage on a small bike powered by a De Dion–Bouton gas motor. The boys were fascinated by both the beautiful woman and her amazing machine. They talked of nothing else during their walk home.

Just a few days later, Bill and Arthur began talking with other workers at the factory about their dream of building a motorcycle engine. A young German **draftsman** named Emil Krueger offered his help. Krueger had seen De Dion–Bouton motors up close and knew a great deal about them. He helped Bill Harley draw a detailed picture of an engine. This first sketch still exists today. It is the earliest recorded history of the Harley-Davidson motorcycle company.

WHI IMAGE ID 6776

Draftsmen carefully sketch out new machine designs.

draftsman: a person who draws designs, often for machinery

2

From Sketch to Machine

Once Bill Harley and Arthur Davidson became serious about building a motorcycle in late 1901, they thought of little else. Both young men worked long hours at the electric motor factory. When they weren't on the job, they were tinkering away in the Davidsons' basement. Bill drew the engineering designs for their future motorcycle. Arthur made the parts by hand using a lathe and a **drill press.** They had recently turned 20 years old, they had no engineering books, and neither had ever been to college. Yet 2 years later, they were riding their first motorcycle.

How could 2 men with such limited **resources** and knowledge build a working motorcycle engine in such a short period of time? They were curious learners, and they looked for clues to solve their design problems. They listened to others and experimented until they got it right. Bill Harley and

drill press: a machine in which a drill is pressed down using a hand lever   **resource:** a source of supply or support

This machine shop contains drill presses, lathes, and other powerful tools.

his work partner Emil Krueger spent many hours together discussing motorcycle engines.

Arthur sought advice from his friend Ole Evinrude, who had moved to Milwaukee and was experimenting with gasoline engines of his own. Evinrude had already built his own car from the ground up. Arthur greatly respected Ole, about whom it was said, "What Ole didn't know about engines no one knew."

Evinrude shared many of his design ideas with Arthur and Bill. In fact, Evinrude's earliest boat motor engine had many similarities to the earliest Harley-Davidson engines. Without his advice and knowledge, it is unlikely the Harley-Davidson motorcycle could have traveled so quickly from paper to reality.

Ole Evinrude with an early boat motor

When they needed better tools, Arthur and Bill turned to their friend Henry Melk. Melk lived a couple of miles away from the Davidsons on the north side of Milwaukee. In his basement he had important tools, such as a drill press for drilling holes in metal, a lathe for crafting precise metal parts, and a noisy gasoline engine that powered the tools. All of these tools were old. Arthur later remembered that the gasoline engine was "persistent in quitting whenever you needed it most."

Arthur and Bill made regular trips to Henry's house, where they probably kept his parents awake with their late-night efforts. Melk's only demand in return: a complete set of parts for the finished engine so that he could build his own motorcycle.

Building that first engine was **tedious** (**tee** dee us) and frustrating work. Arthur Davidson spent many hours shaping the tiny parts that had to fit perfectly together for the engine to work properly. A gasoline motor is very complicated. Energy is created by tiny explosions when gasoline and air are tightly **compressed** in a cylinder by the **piston**, a piece of metal that slides up and down inside of the engine. The piston moves when air in the cylinder is ignited by an electric spark. Each explosion pushes the piston rod down, which turns the **crankshaft**. The crankshaft is connected to the **transmission** (trans **mish** un), which turns the back wheel of the motorcycle and pushes the machine forward.

tedious: tiring because of length or dullness   **compressed:** pressed together
piston: a cylinder-shaped piece of metal that moves up and down in the engine to create the energy that turns the wheels   **crankshaft:** a cylinder-shaped bar made up of a series of bent pieces of metal to which the rods of an engine are attached   **transmission:** the system of gears by which the engine moves the wheels

A Look Inside the Harley-Davidson 8-Valve Racer

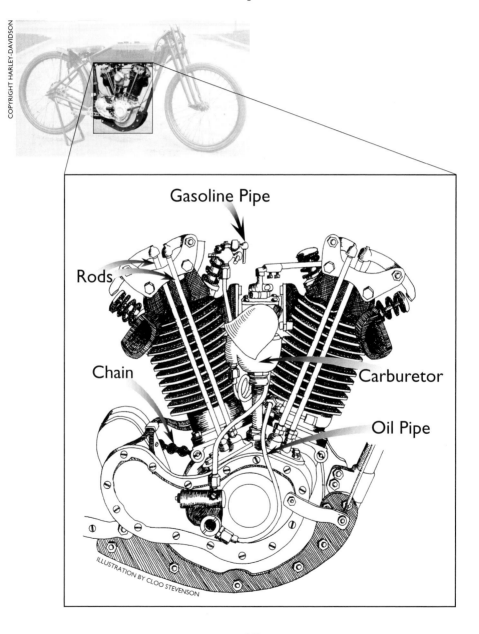

Gasoline Pipe

Rods

Chain

Carburetor

Oil Pipe

ILLUSTRATION BY CLOO STEVENSON

Getting all of these parts to work together was extremely difficult. One of the hardest parts to build was the **carburetor** (**car** buh ray tur). A carburetor mixes gasoline and air together before they are fed into the cylinder, where the piston does its work. If too much gasoline or too much air is used, the engine will shut off.

Bill and Arthur called their first carburetor the "tomato can" because it looked like the tin cans of vegetables in Mrs. Davidson's pantry. There were so few gasoline motors at that time that gas stations didn't exist yet. When they needed fuel for their carburetor, the inventors bought pints of gasoline at the local drugstore.

Finally, after 2 years of hard work, Bill and Arthur had dozens of parts, but they were unable to fit them into a working engine. After laboring away so many late nights and weekends when they could have been relaxing, they still couldn't get the engine to work. Less dedicated inventors would have quit and gone back to fishing. Not Bill and Arthur. Instead of giving up, they looked for more help.

carburetor: the part of the engine used for mixing proper amounts of gasoline and air before they go into the engine

By this time, Arthur's older brother Walter was a skilled **machinist** (muh **shee** nist) who built all kinds of complicated machines and parts for railroad locomotives. The only problem was that Walter was working for the famous Katy Road railway in Parsons, Kansas, more than 500 miles away. How could he possibly help from such a great distance?

Walter Davidson wearing his motorcycle goggles

Arthur dreamed up a clever way around this problem. His oldest brother William's wedding was in April. Why not write Walter about their project and promise him a ride on the motorcycle when he got to Milwaukee?

Their plan worked. From Arthur's letter, Walter must have figured the project was well on its way. He quit his job and hurried home to Milwaukee a few days before the wedding, hoping to get in on the final preparations. He must have

machinist: a person who puts together machines made of metal

been surprised to see a pile of parts all over the Davidsons' basement. He couldn't believe Arthur and Bill hadn't made more progress on the motorcycle.

Once Walter calmed down, Arthur challenged him by saying, "If you can do better, then go to it!" Luckily for everyone, Walter rarely refused a challenge, especially one that had to do with machines. He agreed to help make the project happen.

Walter had always been the most energetic of the Davidson boys. During his teenage years, Walter taught himself about electricity and performed complex experiments in the family basement. At age 17 he became interested in bicycle racing. He frequently took his bike apart and put it together again in the family kitchen to make sure it was in top working order. He trained for races by riding to Madison from Milwaukee, a 75-mile trip that Walter bragged he could make in less than 10 hours.

Walter now focused this fantastic energy and creativity on the motorcycle project. After William's wedding, Walter took a job at the Milwaukee Road railcar shops and moved back into

Although deserted today, the Milwaukee Road railcar shops were busy when the 2 older Davidsons and their father worked there.

the Davidson family home. The basement experiments began again, and Mrs. Davidson was soon complaining about the noise and the grime her sons continually tracked in and out of the house.

It got worse. One day the gasoline fumes from a carburetor experiment met with the open flames used for cooking in the kitchen. With a flash, the cooking fire in the kitchen exploded, knocking over pots and pans. Luckily, the house did not burn down, but Mrs. Davidson was at her limit.

Mrs. Davidson told her husband, "You will have to do something about all this mess in the basement. I won't put up with it any longer!" Mr. Davidson did not like to see his wife unhappy. He built a 10-foot-by-15-foot wooden shed in the backyard. Their sister Janet painted "Harley-Davidson Motor Co." on the door, and the boys were back in business.

Many people have wondered why the founders decided to name their new company Harley-Davidson instead of Davidson-Harley. After all, once William A. officially joined in on the project in 1907, there were 3 Davidsons—Arthur, Walter, and William—and only one Harley. Some people believe that because Bill Harley drew the first designs, it was decided that his name should come first. Others believe that Harley-Davidson just sounded better. We will never know for sure. We do know that all 4 young men were very excited to have their own small factory to finish their first motorcycle.

WHI IMAGE ID 4394

The original woodshed shop where the first Harley-Davidson motorcycles were constructed was in the Davidson family's backyard.

Finally, in the summer of 1903, that first motorcycle was built. Walter demanded the first ride. It is hard to imagine how proud the founders must have felt to see their first motorcycle putter down the street after so much hard work.

Unfortunately, that first machine was not the **reliable** vehicle Harley and the Davidsons had imagined. The engine was too small, just under 2 horsepower. That is less powerful than many leaf blowers are today. The motorcycle struggled up hills and had very little speed. The carburetor did not work well, and the engine did not fit well into the diamond-shaped bicycle frame. Soon it would be back to the shed where work would begin on a bigger and better Harley-Davidson motorcycle.

reliable: does not break down easily

3

Improvements and Innovations

Bill Harley and the Davidson brothers were not easily discouraged. Their first motorcycle was a disappointment, so they began working almost immediately on a new one. Their **innovations** (in oh **vay** shuns) would pave the way for a better, more reliable machine.

At this same time, Bill faced a difficult decision. He wanted to go to college. Unfortunately, his partners needed his knowledge and drawing ability to help them develop a new motorcycle. He had to decide which was more important—staying to help his friends or getting a college education.

After a lot of thought, Bill decided to go to college. He knew that getting a college degree would make him a better motorcycle designer and would help make Harley-Davidson more successful in the long run. Besides, the college he

innovation: a new idea, method, or device

wanted to go to was in Madison, only 75 miles away. He could return home on weekends and during the summer to help his friends.

Bill enrolled at the University of Wisconsin in Madison, where he learned **mechanical engineering** (muh **kan** uh kul en juh **nirh** ing). There was only one class about gasoline engines at that time,

In 1907, Bill Harley graduated from the University of Wisconsin in Madison. This is how the campus looked when he was there.

but Bill learned a lot about design and mechanics at the university. He stayed busy working as a waiter near campus, but he always found time to work on his own engine designs. By winter break, he had plans for a larger, 3¼-horsepower engine that would increase the speed and power of Harley-Davidson motorcycles.

mechanical engineering: a job where you design tools, machinery, and factories

The Davidsons stayed in close contact with Bill while he was away at school. Arthur visited often. One time some students from Purdue University mistook Arthur for a Purdue football star and took Arthur and Bill out for a wild night of fun. Arthur later said it was "as near as I ever got to college."

More often, Arthur's college visits were spent discussing progress on the newest motorcycle. He brought Bill's latest engine designs back to Milwaukee, where he and Walter began work on their next motorcycle in their backyard woodshed factory. Badly in need of parts, they turned to their brother William for help.

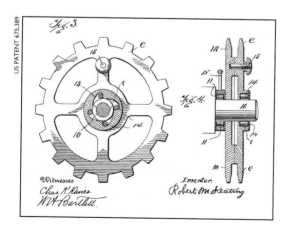

Engineers drew detailed designs for each motorcycle part before it was made.

William was the **foreman** of the Milwaukee Road railway tool shops where parts were made for railroad engines and railroad cars. He wanted to help his brothers, but he had little time to

foreman: the person in charge of a group of workers

spare beyond his job and his new wife at home. It must have been frustrating to watch his brothers work on such an exciting project while he was stuck at the railroad shops. William brought spare parts such as scraps of tubing and leftover metal pieces to the woodshed, where his brothers turned them into pistons, **flywheels**, and other pieces for their motorcycles. It is possible William even built motorcycle parts at the railroad shop using the machines there.

The founders wanted their new motorcycle to be the best in the world. They decided that by combining the best features of all the motorcycles on the market, they could create a great Harley-Davidson motorcycle. Since they couldn't visit all of the other motorcycle companies, they looked through catalogs from the companies for ideas.

Several motorcycle manufacturers were already selling their machines. They were way ahead of Harley-Davidson. Most of these companies were owned by older men with more experience and knowledge than Bill Harley and the Davidson brothers.

flywheel: a wheel used to control the speed of an engine

Indian motorcycles of Springfield, Massachusetts, were the first to go into **mass production**. They were making motorcycles on the East Coast by 1902. The Mitchell motorcycle company was selling cycles in nearby Racine, Wisconsin, and a man named Joseph Merkel was producing them just a few miles away on the south side of Milwaukee. All of these companies created advertisements to help sell their machines.

What does this advertisement claim?

When they looked at these other motorcycles, one thing the Harley-Davidson founders did not like was the bicycle frame, which was shaped like an upside-down diamond. The heavy engine was placed high on the frame, which made it difficult for the rider to balance the cycle. The engine also did not fit easily into the space between the motorcycle seat and the pedals.

mass production: making many of the same item at once using factory machines

Instead, the Harley-Davidson founders adopted the idea of a loop frame that their fellow Milwaukee manufacturer Joseph Merkel was using. The 1903 Merkel frame looped around the engine, allowing the engine to rest securely on the motorcycle. The engine was lower to the ground, and the rider was better balanced.

Indian motorcycles (left) had a diamond-shaped frame, while Merkels (right) had a loop frame.

The founders solved many of the other problems they had experienced with their first motorcycle. Their new motorcycle had a stronger **fork**, the important metal piece that connects the front wheel to the handlebars. They also designed sturdier handlebars and a better carburetor. All of these improvements made the earliest Harley-Davidsons safer and more reliable.

fork: the piece of metal that connects the front wheel of a bicycle or motorcycle to the handlebars

The final touch was adding Bill Harley's bigger and more powerful new engine. Motorcycle riders were embarrassed when they had to get off

The 1905 issue of *Automobile Review* had pictures of some of the earliest Harley-Davidson models.

their machines and walk up steep hills. Some motorcycles, like the Merkel, could reach speeds of only about 35 miles per hour. This new Harley-Davidson engine was powerful enough to get up hills and to move riders along at up to 50 miles per hour.

Bill Harley and the Davidson brothers liked their new design so much that they soon began thinking about producing and selling their machines. One problem remained. How could they possibly build enough motorcycles to make money if their only tools were at Henry Melk's house? They needed their own tools, but they didn't have the money to buy them.

The problem was solved when James McLay, Arthur's uncle, visited the Davidsons from his home in Madison. Uncle James had never married, and he was known for his curious ways. He raised bees in his backyard and shot squirrels out of his bedroom window. A somewhat grumpy and private person, Uncle James loved his nephews' motorcycle project and offered to help. He had saved up a little money over the years and loaned $170 to the Harley-Davidson Motor Company. That doesn't sound like a lot of money today, but his loan probably helped the founders buy a lathe, a drill press, and a gasoline engine to run their new machines. Because of his generosity, James McLay became known as "Honey Uncle." Walter later named his son Gordon McLay Davidson in his uncle's honor.

In 1903, the Harley-Davidson company sold their very first machine to their friend Henry Meyer. He hated the walk to work and begged them to sell him one. Henry Meyer's first Harley-Davidson had an amazingly long life. It lasted through 3 owners and 100,000 miles! Not bad for a group of young men working in a tiny backyard woodshed.

COPYRIGHT HARLEY-DAVIDSON

A picture of one of the first Harley-Davidsons, from 1903 or 1904

These 1904 motorcycles were a great success. They ran well and had enough power to go up steep hills. The founders had the machinery to produce more motorcycles of quality and the talent to keep perfecting their design. Now they just needed the space to build, the time to work, and enough customers to buy their machines as soon as they were produced.

They created more space by doubling the size of their factory, which now took up a large part of the Davidsons' backyard. Walter quit his job at the railroad, and soon after that, Arthur quit working as a pattern maker. Both men could now devote all of their time and energy to making motorcycles. To find customers, Harley-Davidson began advertising in magazines such as *Horseless Age* and *Motorcycle Review*. The Harley-Davidson Motor Company was off and running!

3¾ B. H. P. 3⅛x3½

MOTOR CYCLE MOTORS
One-Piece Cylinder, Lugs cast on casing ready to clamp in frame.
Harley-Davidson Motor Co.
315 Thirty-seventh Street
Milwaukee, Wis.

The founders must have been proud when their first ad was published in *Cycle and Automobile Trade Journal* in January of 1905.

4

A Race for the Top

By 1906 the Harley-Davidson company was going strong. The young businessmen produced 7 or 8 motorcycles in 1905 and then cranked out 50 the following year. They needed a lot of customers to buy up all these machines.

The company attracted many new customers by winning motorcycle races. In some of the first races, Harley-Davidson riders did not do well. They knew very little about racing and lost badly to riders on Mitchell and Indian motorcycles.

Racers crouched low over their handlebars to decrease wind resistance.

But it didn't take long for Harley-Davidson riders to catch on. They learned how to **maneuver** (muh **noo** vur) on the difficult racecourses without crashing into other riders. They gradually started winning many of the races they entered. Newspapers across the country reported these victories, and more orders poured in from new Harley-Davidson customers.

Early motorcycle racers needed assistants to push them off at the starting line.

Walter Davidson was one of the best Harley-Davidson racers. He had been competitive ever since he raced his bicycle in high school. He enjoyed taking on more experienced riders, even when they rode more powerful motorcycles. Walter's favorite races were

Large crowds gathered to watch races like this one in Milwaukee.

maneuver: to move skillfully

the 2-day and 3-day **endurance** runs that took riders across hundreds of miles of open country. During these endurance races, riders were required to follow strict schedules. They had to reach checkpoints at specific times. Each rider started with 1,000 points. Every time he reached a checkpoint too early or too late he lost points. There were also secret checkpoints along the way. Judges were stationed on hills to make sure that riders didn't pedal to help themselves up the steepest parts. Other judges jumped out from hiding places with flags and tested how fast riders could stop.

COPYRIGHT HARLEY-DAVIDSON

Racers sometimes fell backward off of their machines when maneuvering up steep hills.

Endurance races were dangerous. The trails were dotted with rocks, tree roots, and holes that could flatten a tire or send a rider over the handlebars. Riders often ran into one another or crashed into animals blocking the race path. In 1907, Harley-Davidson racer Ralph Sporleder won the medal

endurance: the ability to withstand hard work or stress

38

in an endurance race after running into a stray horse and finishing with a badly bleeding ear. Another rider finally dropped out of a race after 7 flat tires, a lost chain guard, a broken chain, and a dog attack.

In 1906, Walter and 2 other Harley-Davidson riders entered a race sponsored by the Chicago Motorcycle Club. The 2-day race covered 300 miles from Chicago to Milwaukee and back. On the first day of the race, Walter's motorcycle hit a hole in the road and the rear frame broke apart. He was forced to drop out. This was an embarrassing moment and a major disappointment for Walter. He vowed to help create a stronger, more reliable motorcycle and to return for victory in another race.

Walter got his chance in the summer of 1908 during an endurance race in the Catskill Mountains of eastern New York. In the eastern part of the United States, Indian motorcycles were very popular because they were built in Massachusetts. Walter knew that by winning the race he could make people who lived along the East Coast more aware of Harley-

Davidson and challenge Indian for the title of "Best American Motorcycle." Winning would not be easy. The Catskills were much more challenging than the hills around Milwaukee. Walter later described the race route: "Hills did I say? I mean mountains. We westerners don't know what hills are."

Walter Davidson and his teammates, Henry Roberts and F. W. Thomas, at the 1908 National Endurance Contest

Walter and his 2 teammates stuck close together during the race. They helped repair each other's damaged machines and worked as a team to get to the checkpoints on time.

On the first day, Walter stopped during a heavy rainstorm to help his teammate Henry Roberts fix a flat tire. When he finished the tire, he looked at his watch and realized he had only a few minutes to reach the next checkpoint. He raced down a steep hill at top speed. Suddenly his machine hit a bump and leapt into the air. Walter held his breath, praying his frame would not crack and drop him from the race once again. With a thud he hit the ground, shaking his bones and his motorcycle badly. But the frame held, and he covered the final 3 miles in just 3 minutes, barely reaching the checkpoint on time.

During the second day, many riders were forced to drop out because of accidents and broken machines. One rider hit a cow. Another rider fell and bent his frame. A man called "Neverquit" Chadenyne rode more than 60 miles with a broken nose caused by a collision with a milk wagon. Thankfully, Walter Davidson and his teammates finished the race in good condition. Walter was awarded the Diamond Medal and received a perfect 1,000 + 5 score. The extra 5 points were awarded for having almost perfect checkpoint times during the race. By winning the race, Walter had defeated Indian motorcycles and put Harley-Davidson motorcycles into the spotlight.

Walter's victory was a big boost for Harley-Davidson. The race also caused some bad reports about Indian motorcycles.

Walter Davidson was the best endurance racer in the country in 1908.

Reporters from a local newspaper told how Indian riders had camped along the race route a few days before the race and practiced riding the most difficult parts of the course. They also reported that Indian president George Hendee and an employee had followed their riders in an automobile filled with repair equipment and food. Many readers considered this unsportsmanlike, and it hurt Indian's reputation. Walter's team had received no help and finished the race with 2 flat tires but no major repairs.

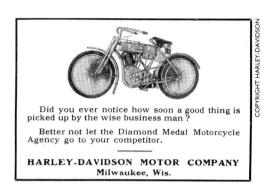

Did you ever notice how soon a good thing is picked up by the wise business man?

Better not let the Diamond Medal Motorcycle Agency go to your competitor.

HARLEY-DAVIDSON MOTOR COMPANY
Milwaukee, Wis.

Harley-Davidson used Walter's racing victories to help sell motorcycles.

The victory demonstrated that Harley-Davidson motorcycles were just as strong and reliable as advertised.

Walter's races definitely increased sales, but many people were not convinced that motorcycles were safe and practical. Doubters called them "devil wagons" or "ugly insects." Many considered them too noisy and dangerous for reliable travel. In the country, riders dealt with bad roads filled with ruts and rocks. When it rained or snowed, motorcycles slid and crashed on the muddy dirt roads. Although motorcycles moved fast, many people thought it was safer to travel by horse or by foot.

WHI IMAGE ID 5499

This calf looks ready for a quick ride to town.

In cities there were other dangers. That's because early motorcycles didn't have a **clutch** to allow a motorcycle to keep running while waiting at a stop sign. When a rider wanted to stop, he or she had to turn off the engine and then run with the motorcycle to get it started again.

The result was often disaster. Riders avoided stopping by racing through stoplights and busy intersections without bothering to follow traffic laws. These risky riders weaved around cars, pedestrians, and horses at high speeds. Sometimes they crashed into innocent bystanders. People learned to run for the sidewalk when they heard a motorcycle coming.

clutch: a device that connects and disconnects the engine to the wheels and transmission

To change people's minds about the "danger" of motorcycles, Harley-Davidson advertised their practical side. New advertisements talked about how owning a motorcycle could help a farmer get to town quickly for a doctor. They mentioned how door-to-door salesmen, bill collectors, and postmen could

Horses could not compete with the ease and convenience of a Harley.

use motorcycles to get around quickly and cheaply. Harley-Davidson also began approaching police departments about buying them for their officers.

Good advertisements and a winning race strategy were beginning to pay off. Harley-Davidson was catching up with Indian and the other major motorcycle companies. The next step was to expand the factory and to set up **dealerships** in different parts of the country.

Harley-Davidsons soon became a common sight on the nation's roads.

dealership: a business that is allowed to sell a certain company's products

5

A Corporation Is Born

All of the hard work was worth it. The many long days in the backyard factory and on the racetrack had pushed Harley-Davidson into the national spotlight. Now it was time for Bill Harley and the Davidson brothers to take advantage of their popularity and expand Harley-Davidson into America's greatest motorcycle company.

WHI IMAGE ID 3251

Young men enjoyed getting together with their motorcycles.

In September of 1907, Harley-Davidson became an official **corporation** in the state of Wisconsin. Harley-Davidson could now sell stock to people who wanted to **invest** in the company. A **share of stock** is a very small portion of what a company is worth. If you buy stock, you're known as a **shareholder**, someone who has invested in the company. If the company makes money, you also make money; if the company loses money, you also lose money. Investing in stock is full of risks, but it can also lead to great wealth. For Harley-Davidson, the more the value of their stock increased, the more money they could use to buy parts, pay employees, and pay for advertising.

The founders held their first official company meeting in their new wooden factory on Chestnut Avenue in Milwaukee, just a few blocks from the Davidson family home. The meeting was held not in a fancy **boardroom** but on the factory floor with machines and parts all around. At the meeting, the founders had to decide who would lead the company. This wasn't easy—everyone, especially Arthur Davidson and Bill Harley, was important to the company's future. Eventually,

corporation: a business that is organized legally   **invest:** to put money into a business in order to make more money   **share of stock:** a small portion of what a company is worth   **shareholder:** a person who has invested money to buy shares of stock in a company   **boardroom:** a room that is used for meetings of a group of people who run a company

they elected Walter as president, Bill Harley as vice president, and Arthur as secretary and treasurer. William Davidson agreed to be **floor manager** of the new factory.

Next they had to decide how much each share of their stock should be worth. They agreed that one stock share would cost $100. Once the first share price was set up,

These workers are using drill presses to make holes in new motorcycle parts.

the price of the stock would go up and down on the **stock market** according to how well the bikes sold. All 4 men had carefully saved their money and bought the first available Harley-Davidson shares. Bill bought 5 shares for $500, William 40 shares for $4,000, Arthur 47 shares for $4,700, and Walter 50 shares for $5,000. This was quite a lot of money to have

floor manager: the person responsible for the machines and workers in a factory   **stock market:** a place where stocks and shares in companies are bought and sold

saved up at that time. In today's dollars, the 4 men had saved nearly $300,000!

One of the other early shareholders was the Davidsons' sister Elizabeth Davidson, sometimes called Bessie. She worked at the factory keeping track of company records. To thank her for all of her hard work, her brothers later paid for her college education.

From left to right: Arthur Davidson, Walter Davidson, Bill Harley, and William Davidson standing outside their offices in Milwaukee

Each of the company founders, Bill Harley and the 3 Davidsons, Arthur, Walter, and William, played a special part in the company. Here's what each contributed.

Arthur Davidson (1881–1950)

Arthur Davidson enjoyed meeting new people. He was a great storyteller and loved to tell funny tales. One time as a joke, Arthur dressed up in a **kilt** and pretended to be a famous Scottish singer named Sir Harry Lauder. People from all over Wisconsin came to see him perform. He did such a great job singing and entertaining the crowd that no one ever knew it was a trick.

Arthur Davidson

Arthur's friendly personality also made him a great salesman. He traveled around the country convincing motorcycle dealers to sell Harley-Davidsons. He soon had dealers in many of the nearby cities, including Chicago, Detroit, and Minneapolis.

kilt: a knee-length skirt worn by men in Scotland

COPYRIGHT HARLEY-DAVIDSON

Arthur could often be found with his suitcase and overcoat, ready for another trip to sell motorcycles.

After Walter's victory in the 1908 New York endurance race, Arthur began promoting Harley-Davidson on the East Coast. Arthur told stories about Walter's races and reminded people that Harley-Davidson had defeated Indian and all of the other motorcycle companies.

Arthur soon had dealers in Boston, Philadelphia, and New York. Indian motorcycles could no longer claim they owned the motorcycle market in the East. Arthur did his best to keep his dealers happy. He knew that dealers who liked their work would sell more motorcycles. His motto was, "Our dealers must make money, and then so will we." He listened to dealers' problems and did his best to help them fix anything that wasn't going well with their dealership.

Some dealerships sold motorcycles and bicycles at the same time.

Arthur eventually opened Harley-Davidson dealerships across the country and soon expanded into foreign countries. By the 1920s, Harley-Davidsons were sold in 67 countries. Arthur had sold motorcycles as far away as Australia and Japan. Thanks to his efforts, the name of Harley-Davidson was known not just in the United States, but all over the world. Arthur's business sense helped the company sell machines in places the 4 founders probably never dreamed of when they first started.

Walter Davidson (1876–1942)

The founders soon discovered that Walter was more than just a motorcycle racer. He had a great head for business and made an excellent company president. He was extremely energetic and hardworking. Walter's wife, Emma, complained she was lucky if he was home by 8:00 p.m. on Christmas Eve. In fact, all of

COPYRIGHT HARLEY-DAVIDSON

Walter Davidson

the founders worked incredibly hard. They often stayed at the factory until 10:00 p.m., even on Sundays.

Walter was a perfectionist. He wanted to make sure Harley-Davidson produced the best-quality motorcycles in the world. He test-drove each new motorcycle on the street behind the factory to make sure it ran perfectly. He sometimes raced beside trains along the railroad tracks to show off the speed of his cycles. If the engine ran rough or the handlebars weren't sturdy, he sent the machine back

Even wearing a suit and tie, Walter loved to test-drive the new motorcycles.

to the factory for improvements. Only motorcycles that met his approval would be sold.

Walter did not allow Harley-Davidson dealers to replace any parts with equipment from other manufacturers. He didn't think parts from other companies were good enough to put on his motorcycles. He also insisted that any **defective** (dih **fek** tiv) parts be replaced for free. He understood that if Harley-Davidson motorcycles were reliable, their customers would remain loyal for many years to come.

Even though Walter believed in producing the best-quality motorcycles, he was very careful with the company's money. He kept detailed records of what the company spent and was constantly looking for places where they could save money.

defective: faulty, doesn't work correctly

55

People sometimes thought he was being a cheapskate, but Walter knew that every penny he saved could be used to make the company bigger and better.

William "Bill" Harley (1880–1943)

Bill Harley graduated from the University of Wisconsin in 1907. He enjoyed his time in college, but he was excited to get back to work designing motorcycles full time. Bill was a quiet and kind person, but just like Walter he was passionate about making great motorcycles. Never satisfied, he could always think of

Bill Harley

some way to make the motorcycles better. Instead of just talking about things he didn't like, Bill took new ideas and immediately started thinking about ways to make them work.

Bill Harley and his team of engineers worked hard to make sure their motorcycles got better every year. One of the improvements they made was to invent a front fork with a spring in it. The fork connects the front wheel to the handlebars, and the spring made riding over bumpy roads much easier on riders. In 1912, the engineers replaced the leather drive belt connecting the engine to the rear wheel with a metal chain. This chain was stronger and less likely to break than the leather belt.

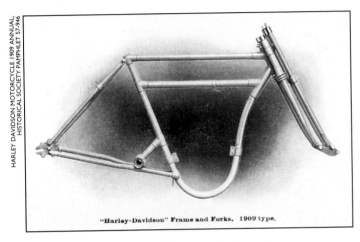

HARLEY DAVIDSON MOTORCYCLE 1909 ANNUAL, HISTORICAL SOCIETY PAMPHLET 57-946

"Harley-Davidson" Frame and Forks. 1909 type.

By 1909, Bill Harley and his team had made many improvements to the original loop frame.

Another problem Harley and his team overcame was getting oil to the engine **efficiently** (ih **fish** unt lee). All gasoline engines need oil to **lubricate** (**loo** bruh kate) the fast-moving metal parts in the engine and keep them from scraping against each other. Early Harley-Davidson motorcycles had oil hand pumps. The riders squeezed a bulb that pushed oil into the engine when they thought it needed

efficiently: without wasting time or energy   **lubricate:** to make smooth or slippery

oil. Some riders pumped oil too often. The extra oil burned off in clouds of black smoke that followed the motorcycles wherever they went. Other riders didn't pump enough oil, which damaged the engines and shortened the lives of their motorcycles. The engineering team solved this problem by developing a mechanical system that put oil into the engine automatically.

When customers demanded more power and speed, Harley's team experimented with a 2-cylinder V-twin engine. The engine earned this nickname because the 2 cylinders came together in a 45-degree angle, making a V shape. These larger engines nearly doubled the motorcycle's power and helped Harley-Davidson compete with other high-powered motorcycle brands. Early models had mechanical problems, but by 1911 the factory was producing many V-twins. The V-twin became a Harley-Davidson trademark and is still used on most of its motorcycles today.

HARLEY DAVIDSON MOTORCYCLE 1909 ANNUAL, HISTORICAL SOCIETY PAMPHLET 57-946

Customers were excited about the V-twin, which featured a powerful 2-cylinder engine in the shape of a V.

William Davidson (1870–1937)

The fourth founder, William Davidson, was the floor supervisor at the factory. He usually kept his office door open so workers could drop in to talk about their problems or just to chat. This often kept William from completing his work, so he developed a way to wrap up conversations and get his visitors out of his office.

William Davidson

He placed a barrel of peanuts beside his office door. When he felt a conversation had gone on too long, he would say, "Do you like peanuts? Grab a handful on your way out."

William worked on the **assembly line** with the employees, building

William Davidson (on the left) loved working on the factory floor with his employees.

assembly line: an arrangement of machines and workers in which work passes from one worker to the next until the product is finished

parts and putting the motorcycles together. His desk was always covered with pieces of machines that didn't work. His earlier experience with the railroads helped him keep the employees organized and working efficiently. Often called "Old Bill," he was well liked by his employees.

An expanded factory could hold dozens of new motorcycles.

William was very generous. He kept a small notebook where he wrote down the names of employees who borrowed money from him. He rarely reminded the employees about these debts and patiently waited until they found enough money to pay him back.

All of Harley-Davidson's founders wanted their motorcycles to be perfect. They did not spend a lot of time worrying about fancy paint jobs or special **accessories** (ak **sess** uh reez) such as those many motorcycles have today. They were mainly concerned that their machines were safe, reliable, comfortable, and powerful. The founders knew that if each of their motorcycles had these 4 qualities, their customers would always remain loyal.

And all of the founders were kind and loyal to their workers. They could often be found on the factory floor in plain blue work shirts just like the other employees wore. They knew their employees well and thought of them as part of the Harley-Davidson family. Once, when an

COPYRIGHT HARLEY-DAVIDSON

Harley-Davidson employees were a dedicated group who believed their motorcycles were the best.

accessory: something that adds to the beauty or effectiveness of an object

employee needed a new home, William helped to purchase lumber and then worked together with other employees to help build the house.

All the employees at Harley-Davidson were expected to work hard and were rewarded for doing so. When a big job was finished, Walter raised a flag above the factory. The founders and employees would stop work and celebrate their accomplishment.

As for their own families, the founders worked so hard they were rarely home to help around the house. But they set up a system. Whenever one of their wives or children needed to go somewhere, an employee was sent from the factory with a motorcycle and sidecar. The Harley-Davidson founders took their work seriously, but they remembered that their families were also important.

Harley-Davidson was becoming a major company. Each year brought more orders from excited customers. Bill Harley and the Davidsons were no longer making motorcycles in their backyard factory, but they were still involved in everything that happened at Harley-Davidson. They knew that if they kept their employees, dealers, customers, and families happy, Harley-Davidson would continue growing for a long time.

By 1909, Harley-Davidson had completed a brick addition to their 2-story wooden factory.

6

Rough Times and Creative Solutions

What amazing growth the company had in just 10 years! By 1914, the company had expanded from a backyard woodshed to a modern red brick factory with more than 2 million square feet of work space—that's 10,000 times bigger than their original backyard shop! More than 1,500 employees cranked out 20,000 motorcycles that year. In 1904 it took the founders nearly 4 months to produce one machine. Now they were rolling out a new Harley-Davidson motorcycle every 5½ minutes! Many of their **competitors**, including Merkel and Mitchell motorcycles, had dropped out of the business. Indian was now Harley-Davidson's only major competitor in the United States. There seemed to be no limit to Harley-Davidson's future.

competitor: a rival or challenger

Look at how Harley-Davidson had expanded its factory by 1919!

The founders no longer had to worry about their tools breaking down. Harley-Davidson employees now worked with the best equipment in the world. The factory's new machines used patterns called **jigs** that directed automatic drills and grinders to cut metal and drill holes in the same exact spot on every part that came down the assembly line. This meant that parts could be made quickly and easily with few mistakes.

jig: a pattern used to guide automatic drills so that the same shape is cut each time

Harley-Davidson riders were very loyal to the company. The motorcycles were called "Silent Gray Fellows" because of their color and their quiet and reliable ride. Advertisements reminded people that Harley-Davidson motorcycles were "built on honor" and were of the best quality. Owners got together in Harley-Davidson clubs to take rides together and talk about their motorcycles. Riders carry on this tradition today with the Harley Owners Group, or HOG, which has club **chapters** all around the country who gather for special meetings and events.

It Rules the Road
The Harley-Davidson
Two-Speed Twin

The most powerful motorcycle manufactured. Eight actual horsepower, 61 cubic inches piston displacement.

This Harley-Davidson is built strong enough for sidecar use. Special brake, special hubs, double control of both clutch and brake. Frame, forks, and all other parts reinforced for sidecar service. Patented Harley-Davidson Step-Starter regular equipment.

New Two-Speed Harley-Davidson Twins will be sold in 1914 thus all other Harley-Davidson models combined.

Phone or call for a demonstration

MUELLER CYCLE COMPANY 724 NATIONAL AVE.

No motorcycles ruled the road like Harley-Davidson.

By 1913, groups like the Chicago Motorcycle Club could be found all over the country.

chapter: a small group in a bigger organization

Just when it looked like everything was going well, the founders were forced into a difficult situation. Harley-Davidson had become popular by winning motorcycle races, but racing suddenly became much more dangerous. The new style of racing was on circular tracks called **motordromes** made of wooden boards. The tracks had very steep sides that helped racers achieve high speeds. These boards quickly rotted and cracked because of the heavy pounding of the motorcycles. Oil from the racers' machines spilled onto the track, making it slippery. Even worse, the racing bikes had no brakes and almost nothing to absorb the shock of a bumpy ride or to protect riders from bouncing around. Many riders were injured or killed in horrible crashes during these **boardtrack races**.

Boardtrack racers risked their lives to win races.

The founders, especially Arthur, wondered if Harley-Davidson should support such a dangerous sport. Arthur

motordrome: a circular, wooden racing track with steep sides so riders can achieve high speeds
boardtrack race: a race that takes place on circular, wooden motordrome tracks

67

called these racetracks "murderdromes" because of their ability to take racers' lives. "The killing of a half a dozen riders every season and the occasional killing of a few **spectators** (**spek** tay turz) does motorcycling positive injury instead of benefit," Arthur argued.

Harley-Davidson refused to enter boardtrack races for several years. But the problem did not go away. Boardtrack racing gained popularity, and many racers who didn't work for the company rode on Harley-Davidson motorcycles anyway. Indian motorcycles were winning races, and the founders feared they would lose customers if they didn't compete.

In 1914 they agreed to get back into racing. Bill Harley established a racing department at the company and created a series of machines built for the high-speed motordromes. Arthur and the other founders were still concerned that their racers would be injured, so they encouraged using smaller, one-cylinder engines that didn't reach such high speeds. Eventually the rules were changed so that these smaller, safer engines were the only type allowed.

spectator: a person who watches but does not participate, as at a sports event

The new racing team immediately began winning. From 1914 through 1921 they dominated racing events across the country. The Harley-Davidson racing team was called the "Wrecking Crew" because they destroyed the chances of any team that competed against them.

Why was motorcycle racing so popular during these years? Perhaps it was a **diversion** (dih **vur** zhuhn) from the horrors of World War I,

The Dodge City Wrecking Crew rarely lost a race.

which broke out in Europe in 1914. The United States joined the fight against Germany and Austro-Hungary in 1917. As a result, motorcycle sales to American customers dropped off sharply during these years. People had little time to think about the pleasures of motorcycling when thousands of soldiers were being killed in the war trenches every day.

diversion: an activity that relaxes or entertains

WHI IMAGE ID 4689

But the war also helped the company. Harley-Davidson became involved in the war effort by providing nearly 18,000 motorcycles to the U.S. military. American and British soldiers rode specially made Harley-Davidsons during the war to deliver messages or perform scouting missions.

Motorcycles were not just for men. These machines were often equipped with sidecars that carried supplies or could even be mounted with machine guns.

COPYRIGHT HARLEY-DAVIDSON

In fact, World War I created many new customers for Harley-Davidson. Lots of soldiers fell in love with their Harleys and purchased their own when they returned from the war.

World War I introduced Harley-Davidson to thousands of soldiers.

Many of the machines sold to the military stayed in Europe after the war ended. This helped create new customers in France, England, and Italy. After the war, Harley-Davidson dealerships again began to sell motorcycles as quickly as they came off the assembly line in Milwaukee.

But this remarkable growth could not continue forever. For one thing, Indian was attracting customers away from Harley-Davidson with new models and creative advertising schemes. The rising popularity of automobiles was an even bigger problem. Ford cars could be bought for as little as $245. The most expensive Harley-Davidsons cost more than $300. People who couldn't afford cars before were now buying them instead of motorcycles.

Ford cars and trucks were cheap and reliable transportation.

Things got worse in 1920 when the world's economy went through a brief **depression** (dih **presh** un). Motorcycle sales dropped as many people saved their money for more

depression: a period of slow business activity and job loss

71

important things. In 1920 Harley-Davidson produced 28,189 motorcycles. The next year they made only 10,202. This was the first time the company had ever lost so much money. The founders and Harley-Davidson employees were worried.

Tough times got even worse during the Great Depression of the 1930s. When the stock market crashed in 1929, stock investors across the United States lost millions of dollars in just a few days. Companies

The employment office was the first stop for men who lost their jobs during the Great Depression.

closed down, and millions of people lost their jobs. People all around the world feared that things might never be the same again.

Although motorcycles had been fun to drive when people had extra money to spend, they were a luxury few people could afford during a depression. In 1933, Harley-Davidson produced only 3,703 motorcycles. This was the lowest number since 1910, when the company was just getting started. The founders thought seriously about shutting down the factory.

But they weren't quitters. After talking it over, they decided they couldn't give up on their company because of a few difficult years. They determined to get all of their best employees together and develop creative ways to attract new customers. Money might be scarce, but they knew there must be some way to keep people buying their products.

Harley-Davidson had always worked hard to keep their customers happy. They often adapted their machines for all kinds of special requests. Their sidecars could be designed to carry groceries, deliver mail, haul farm supplies, and even transport caskets for funeral homes. Their motors had been used on boats, homemade cars, airplanes, and even bowling ball polishing machines. Harley-Davidson also produced a line of bicycles for a few years.

Sidecars and Service Vehicles

Sidecars helped Harley-Davidson prove that motorcycles were just as useful as any car or truck. They could carry an extra person or be used to carry heavy loads. Sidecars that could transport an extra person were called "pal cars" or "chummy cars" and came with special coverings so passengers could stay warm and dry in bad weather. The first delivery motorcycle, made in 1915, had a wooden container with a hinged lid mounted on its sidecar. A special department at the Milwaukee factory painted signs for "Al's Meat Market" or "East Side Plumbing Supplies" on the delivery vehicles before sending them out to their customers.

Many businesses preferred Harley-Davidsons to horse drawn carriages or Ford cars because they were easy to manage on bumpy country roads and were not too expensive to keep up. One Harley-Davidson ad reminded customers that motorcycles got much better gas mileage than trucks: "Don't use trucks for delivery. You're carting away profits with every trip. Use a Harley-Davidson."

This sidecar provided road service for broken down cars.

74

The founders now expanded on their creativity. To find new customers, they gave out special books where Harley-Davidson owners could write down names of friends they thought might want to buy a motorcycle. If 8 people from the list bought a motorcycle, the rider received a gold medal and $500 in cash.

The founders saved money by taking parts from leftover machines to create a small and inexpensive new motorcycle called the Model B. This model cost $195, one of the cheapest Harley-Davidsons ever. They sold more than 1,000 of these new machines when sales of their other models were way down.

The 1927 Model B was a great option for motorcycle lovers who didn't have a lot of money.

The company made more money by selling some of their designs to Japan. The Japanese were very interested in motorcycles and soon began building excellent machines of their own. The founders hated to sell their secrets to another country, but they needed the money badly. This money was used to create one of the most famous Harley-Davidson motorcycles of all time. The 1936 Model EL was called the Knucklehead because the metal covers on the sides of the engine looked like the knuckles on a closed fist. This low and powerful machine was fast and beautiful. A Harley-Davidson racer named Joe Petrali drove a Knucklehead 136 miles per hour for a national speed record in 1937. Thousands of riders rushed out to get one for themselves. Harley-Davidson's popularity had returned.

COPYRIGHT HARLEY-DAVIDSON

The founders were proud of the popular 1936 EL "Knucklehead."

When World War II broke out in Europe in 1939, Harley-Davidson helped the U.S. military once again. They produced almost 90,000 military motorcycles that were used in battles throughout Europe. Just as they had during World War I, Harley-Davidson won awards from the military for the excellent quality of their machines and for their commitment to the war effort.

Harley-Davidson had survived many difficult years and 2 world wars. But another challenge lay ahead, as the aging founders began to give up control of the company. William Davidson died in 1937, Walter in 1942, Bill Harley in 1943, and finally Arthur in 1950. Now it would be up to their sons to carry on the Harley-Davidson tradition.

7

Past and Present Come Together

It was no surprise that the next generation of Harleys and Davidsons were ready to take over the company when their fathers were ready to pass it on. After all, the founders' sons grew up at the factory sweeping the floors, talking with employees, and checking out the latest motorcycles. They could often be found at motorcycle racetracks and at various Harley-Davidson events. By the time Walter Davidson was nearing his death in 1942, several of the founders' sons were working for the company. As

The founders' sons on their 1930 machines.
From left: Gordon, Allan, Walter C., and William H. Davidson, and John Harley.

company president, he wanted to make sure their future with Harley-Davidson was decided before he died.

According to his granddaughter Jean Davidson, in 1942 Walter gathered the family together in his hospital room, where he announced his plan for the future of the company. William Davidson's son, William H., was a strong leader and a good businessman, just like his uncle Walter. He was Walter's choice for the new company president. Walter's son, Walter C., was friendly and outgoing like his uncle Arthur, so he would become

William H. Davidson was a motorcycle racer like his uncle Walter before he became company president.

head of sales. Walter's other son, Gordon, became the new vice president of manufacturing, and Bill J. Harley replaced his father as vice president of engineering.

This new generation of leaders worked hard and cared about Harley-Davidson just as much as their fathers had. But their abilities would soon be tested by another threat to Harley-Davidson's reputation—the outlaw biker. Following World War II, many former soldiers struggled to fit back into American society. Some of them roamed the country on their motorcycles looking for excitement or just trying to forget about the war. Often these riders **customized (kus** tum ized) their bikes to make themselves more noticeable. They removed the front fenders and front brakes, put on smaller front wheels, and made the bikes louder by removing the mufflers. These low-riding, tough-looking machines were called **bobbers or choppers** because their parts were chopped

and changed around to make them unique. Not all of the choppers were Harley-Davidsons, but many of them were.

People still customize their bikes, like this 1986 Heritage Softail.

customized: changed to suit an individual's needs   **bobbers or choppers:** motorcycles customized by their owners to give them a tough appearance, with large back wheels and a loud engine

Gangs of chopper riders sometimes got into trouble. They rode into small towns with their black leather jackets, raced up and down streets, and sometimes got into fights. In 1947, *Life* magazine reported that a 3-day motorcycle event in a small town called Hollister, California, ended in a major disagreement between the outlaw bikers and everyone else. *Life* described bikers riding wildly through the town, with dozens of people arrested after fights broke out. The magazine story included pictures of outlaw riders and tales of townspeople running for their lives in fear. A few years later, the movie *The Wild One*, starring Marlon Brando, told a similar story about a gang of **rowdy** motorcycle riders. People across the country began to fear the sound of approaching motorcycles in their neighborhoods.

The idea that motorcycle riders were villains bothered the people at Harley-Davidson, especially the new president, William H. Davidson. They fought hard to remind customers that Harley-Davidsons were safe and reliable machines. Their advertisements showed well-dressed people riding their motorcycles to picnics and to the beach. It didn't matter.

rowdy: rough or loud in behavior

81

Much of the public was convinced that motorcycles, especially Harley-Davidsons, were for outlaws only.

No outlaws in this 1950s ad—just a good-looking couple out for a safe ride.

Another problem for Harley-Davidson was foreign **competition** (com puh **tish** un). Indian motorcycles finally closed in 1953, but Harley-Davidson faced more difficult competition from Europe and Japan. Harleys had always been big and powerful motorcycles. Now British companies, such as Triumph and

Japanese motorcycles like Suzuki created competition for Harley-Davidson.

Norton, and Japanese brands, such as Honda and Yamaha, started gaining customers with their smaller and more efficient machines. These foreign bikes were not too

competition: the effort of one company to attract more business than another

82

expensive, drove very smoothly, and didn't break down as often as Harley-Davidsons did.

To compete, Harley-Davidson created smaller bikes, such as the speedy Sportster. The company also produced motorized scooters and even golf carts in hopes of finding new customers. Another solution was to buy half of an Italian company called Aermacchi, which built lightweight, inexpensive motorcycles similar to some of the Hondas.

It wasn't enough. Japanese and British companies got more and more customers each year. Honda took advantage of Harley-Davidson's outlaw reputation with ads that said, "You Meet the Nicest People Riding Hondas." By 1966, Harley-Davidson made only about $30 million a year, while Honda was making more than $100 million. By 1970, only 5 out of 100 motorcycles on the road were Harleys.

The final blow came when Harley-Davidson decided to sell itself to a larger company called American Machine and Foundry (AMF). William H. Davidson retired, and for the first

time neither a Davidson nor a Harley family member ran the
company. It looked like the long family tradition at Harley-
Davidson was over.

Unfortunately, the difficult times for the company
continued, even though it had new owners. During the
1970s, AMF produced motorcycles quickly and cheaply to
keep up with their competitors. Many of the new machines
were made with less quality than the originals. Customers
often returned their brand-new motorcycles because they
broke down or did not run smoothly. Harley-Davidson
employees were not as proud of their work as they had been
when the founders were alive.

And then an amazing thing happened. In 1981, AMF
decided to sell Harley-Davidson because it was not making a
profit. A small group of Harley-Davidson employees, including
William Davidson's grandson, Willie G., pooled together
enough money to buy it back from AMF. Once again, Harley-
Davidson was controlled by family members and people who
truly believed in the company. They celebrated with T-shirts

that read, "The Eagle Soars Alone" to symbolize their new **independence** from AMF.

THE EAGLE SOARS ALONE.

MOTOR HARLEY-DAVIDSON COMPANY

COMMEMORATING THE RETURN
TO PRIVATE OWNERSHIP OF
HARLEY-DAVIDSON MOTOR COMPANY
JUNE, 1981

Harley fans were overjoyed when Willie G. Davidson bought back the company back from AMF in 1981.

Buying back the company was a huge risk. Harley-Davidson had a lot of financial problems and was still far behind the Japanese motorcycle companies. The new owners would have to completely rebuild the company to make it successful again.

Luckily for Willie G. Davidson and his partners, during the 1980s there was a sudden rise in American pride. American President Ronald Reagan encouraged the country to buy American products. Harley-Davidson took advantage by advertising the company's long history as a strong American company. After all, what could be more American than riding

independence: freedom; the ability to work alone

a long stretch of highway on your very own Harley-Davidson motorcycle?

The company produced a new series of bikes called Softails that reminded riders of the most popular models of the 1940s and 1950s. These new machines hid their rear shocks at the bottom of the frame beneath the transmission. They combined the low and fast look of older bikes with the smooth ride of a modern motorcycle. Middle-aged men and women who had ridden Harley-Davidsons in high school or college began buying these new motorcycles with the **vintage** (**vin** tedj) looks.

At the same time, Harley-Davidson improved the quality and efficiency of all of its motorcycles. Company employees visited Honda factories and came home with ideas for how they could use

COPYRIGHT HARLEY-DAVIDSON

Softail bikes combine the best parts of Harley-Davidson's past and present.

vintage: old; from a certain period in the past

Japanese manufacturing methods to improve their products. They cut down on wasted parts, taught their employees to fix their own mistakes, and improved working conditions at their factories. Their new engine, the Evolution, was more powerful and had fewer mechanical problems than anything they had ever produced.

The company quickly became successful again. Old customers returned, and new ones bought up Harley-Davidsons faster than they could be produced. Harley-Davidson has grown tremendously since the early 1980s. Today the company is back on top of the motorcycle market, just as they were during the founders' days.

Willie G. Davidson, a colorful character who collects old Harleys, is still in charge of the styling department and has helped develop many exciting new motorcycles. The latest addition is the V-Rod, a **fuel-injected** machine that was designed with the sports car company Porsche Engineering Services. With the V-Rod, Harley-Davidson can compete with the highest-performing motorcycles in the world. The

fuel-injected: a type of engine in which gasoline is turned into a fine spray and shot directly into the engine's cylinders

COPYRIGHT HARLEY-DAVIDSON

Japanese companies can no longer truthfully argue that Harley-Davidsons are slow and poorly built.

This 2002 V-Rod brings Harley-Davidson technology into the twenty-first century.

Harley-Davidson has never been more popular. Fans buy thousands of leather jackets, coffee mugs, Christmas ornaments, and clocks bearing the company logo. Huge meetings of motorcyclists in Sturgis, South Dakota, and Daytona Beach, Florida, draw hundreds of thousands of

COPYRIGHT HARLEY-DAVIDSON

riders each year. There are Harley-Davidson dealerships in every state, and every dealership sponsors a Harley Owners Group, which brings riders together for social events and scenic rides.

Harley-Davidson dealerships are often crowded with new customers.

Harley-Davidson Rallies

Harley-Davidson owners have always loved getting together for races, group rides, and parties. In 1938 a group of 19 riders called the Jackpine Gypsies roasted a pig and raced their bikes around the desert of Sturgis, South Dakota. Riders have returned to Sturgis every August since. Nowadays as many as 600,000 people from all over the country turn the tiny town of Sturgis into motorcycle headquarters U.S.A. Visitors come for races, bike shows, tattoo contests, motor rodeos, bungee jumping, and other kinds of wild and crazy motorcycle fun. Daytona Beach, Florida, hosts a similar **rally** every March. Policemen from surrounding counties help keep things under control and neighboring towns send garbage men to deal with the 700 tons of

Rallies like this one in Elkhart, Wisconsin, are popular with Harley-Davidson fans.

trash. Nowhere else besides Sturgis and Daytona can you find so many Harley-Davidson fans in the same place at the same time.

rally: a gathering of a large group of people for a specific cause

Some people argue that you can tell Harley-Davidson fans just by what they're wearing. At the Sturgis and Daytona Beach rallies, there are lots of riders wearing black leather jackets and tattoos and riding custom choppers. But Harley-Davidsons are also found in the garages of people who ride to work wearing suits and ties with their motorcycle gear. No matter what type of rider, Harley-Davidson is a popular choice for many Americans and people around the world.

Part of Harley-Davidson's success is due to its loyal customers.

The company has changed a great deal since the days when the Davidson brothers and their friend Bill Harley built each of their machines by hand. Or has it? The V-twin engine first produced in 1909 still powers most Harley-Davidsons today. Many Harley-Davidsons have the same look and sound of machines that were produced more than 50 years ago. The technology has improved, and the company's size has increased, but at its heart Harley-Davidson is still just an American company producing top-quality motorcycles.

Appendix

Harley-Davidson Time Line

1901 — Bill Harley draws his first sketch of a motorcycle engine.

1903 — The first motorcycle is completed.

Arthur Davidson's father builds the boys a backyard woodshed for their motorcycles.

William and Walter Davidson join forces with Bill Harley and Arthur Davidson.

Harley-Davidson sells a motorcycle to friend Henry Meyer.

1906 — Harley-Davidson produces 50 motorcycles.

Work begins on a modern motorcycle factory on Chestnut Avenue in Milwaukee.

1907 — Harley-Davidson becomes an official company and begins selling stock.

1908 — Walter Davidson wins the National Motorcycle Endurance Contest in New York.

1911 — The factory begins producing 2-cylinder V-twin motorcycle engines.

1914 — Harley-Davidson builds 20,000 motorcycles.

1914 — The Harley-Davidson "Wrecking Crew" begins winning motorcycle races all across the country.

1917 — Harley-Davidson begins production of more than 18,000 military motorcycles during World War I.

1929 — The Great Depression begins, and Harley-Davidson sales drop significantly.

1936 — The Knucklehead motorcycle helps Harley-Davidson regain its popularity.

1937 — William Davidson dies.

1939 — Harley-Davidson begins production of almost 90,000 motorcycles for the U.S. and British military during World War II.

1942 — Walter Davidson names the next generation of Harley-Davidson leaders.

Walter Davidson dies.

1943 — Bill Harley dies.

1950 — Arthur Davidson dies.

1953 — Harley-Davidson's competitor, Indian motorcycles, shuts down.

1969 — Harley-Davidson is sold to American Machine and Foundry (AMF).

1981 — Grandson Willie G. Davidson and partners buy back Harley-Davidson from AMF.

2003 — Harley-Davidson celebrates its 100th birthday and is once again on top of the motorcycle market.

Glossary

accessory (ak **sess** uh ree): something that adds to the beauty or effectiveness of an object

adapted: changed for a particular use or situation

assembly line: an arrangement of machines and workers in which work passes from one worker to the next until the product is finished

boardroom: a room that is used for meetings of a group of people who run a company

boardtrack race: a race that takes place on circular, wooden motordrome tracks

bobbers or choppers: motorcycles customized by their owners to give them a tough appearance, with large back wheels and a loud engine

brewery (**broo** ur ee): a factory that produces beer

carburetor (**car** buh ray tur): the part of the engine used for mixing proper amounts of gasoline and air before they go into the engine

casting: an object cast or created in a mold

chapter: a small group in a bigger organization

clutch: a device that connects and disconnects the engine to the wheels and transmission

competition (com puh **tish** un): the effort of one company to attract more business than another

competitor: a rival or challenger

compressed: pressed together

corporation: a business that is organized legally

crankshaft: a cylinder-shaped bar made up of a series of bent pieces of metal to which the rods of an engine are attached

customized (**kus** tum ized): changed to suit an individual's needs

dealership: a business that is allowed to sell a certain company's products

defective (dih **fek** tiv): faulty, doesn't work correctly

depression (dih **presh** un): a period of slow business activity and job loss

diversion (dih **vur** zhuhn): an activity that relaxes or entertains

draftsman: a person who draws designs, often for machinery

drill press: a machine in which a drill is pressed down using a hand lever

efficiently (ih **fish** unt lee): without wasting time or energy

endurance: the ability to withstand hard work or stress

floor manager: the person responsible for the machines and workers in a factory

flywheel: a wheel used to control the speed of an engine

foreman: the person in charge of a group of workers

fork: the piece of metal that connects the front wheel of a bicycle or motorcycle to the handlebars

fuel-injected: a type of engine in which gasoline is turned into a fine spray and shot directly into the engine's cylinders

horsepower: a unit for measuring the power of an engine

independence: freedom; the ability to work alone

innovation (in oh **vay** shun): a new idea, method, or device

invest: to put money into a business in order to make more money

iron foundry: a factory that melts and shapes metal

jig: a pattern used to guide automatic drills so that the same shape is cut each time

kilt: a knee-length skirt worn by men in Scotland

lathe (layth): a machine in which a piece of wood or metal is held and turned while being shaped by a tool

lubricate (**loo** bruh kate): to make smooth or slippery

machinist (muh **shee** nist): a person who puts together machines made of metal

maneuver (muh **noo** vur): to move skillfully

manufacturer (man yoo **fak** chur ur): a company that makes something, often using machines

mass production: making many of the same item at once using factory machines

mechanical engineering (muh **kan** uh kul en juh **nihr** ring): a job where you design tools, machinery, and factories

motordrome: a circular, wooden racing track with steep sides so riders can achieve high speeds

outboard motor: a motor with a propeller that can be attached to the rear of a small boat

pattern maker: a person who shapes wood to make patterns for machine parts

piston: a cylinder-shaped piece of metal that moves up and down in the engine to create the energy that turns the wheels

produced: made, put together

rally: a gathering of a large group of people for a specific cause

reliable: does not break down easily

resource: a source of supply or support

rowdy: rough or loud in behavior

share of stock: a small portion of what a company is worth

shareholder: a person who has invested money to buy shares of stock in a company

spectator (**spek** tay tur): a person who watches but does not participate, as at a sports event

stock market: a place where stocks and shares in companies are bought and sold

tedious (**tee** dee us): tiring because of length or dullness

transmission (trans **mish** un): the system of gears by which the engine moves the wheels

vintage (**vin** tedj): old; from a certain period in the past

Reading Group Guide and Activities

Discussion Questions

🐾 Harley-Davidson became a successful company even though there were many other companies that also made motorcycles. Why do you think Harley-Davidson sold more and more motorcycles while other companies such as Mitchell, Merkel, and Indian motorcycles lost their customers and had to give up?

🐾 Bill Harley had to choose between staying in Milwaukee to help his friends improve their motorcycle and going to college in Madison. Do you think he made the right choice? Why or why not?

🐾 During the Great Depression, Harley-Davidson lost many of its customers because people did not have enough money to buy motorcycles. If you were in charge of the company, what would you have done to help sell more motorcycles?

🐾 Arthur Davidson did not want Harley-Davidson motorcycles to race at the motordrome because many racers were injured or killed during these races. Harley-Davidson eventually decided to start racing because all of the other motorcycle companies had racing teams. Why do you think the company made that decision? Do you agree or disagree with it?

🐾 Each of the 4 founders of Harley-Davidson had special skills that they used to make their company successful. Look back at Chapter 5, and discuss what was special about each founder and how they used their talents to help Harley-Davidson succeed.

Activities

- Vice president Willie G. Davidson is looking for ideas for a new Harley-Davidson motorcycle. Draw a picture of your best design idea. Make sure to label the important parts and describe how your motorcycle is different from any other.

- Your reading group is in charge of creating a new commercial to help sell Harley-Davidson motorcycles. Write out what you will say, and then perform the commercial for your class. Make sure to include a catchy slogan or a jingle that will make people excited about Harley-Davidson. If more than one of you performs, create a skit where each of you plays a different role.

- Arthur Davidson and Bill Harley fulfilled their dreams by creating their very own motorcycle company. To achieve this, they had to go step-by-step, never losing sight of their goal. What is your dream? What steps do you need to take to get there? Write about your dream and how you could make it become real.

- Some states require motorcycle riders to wear helmets, and other states do not. Research which states have helmet laws. Do you think motorcycle riders should be required to wear helmets? Develop a list of reasons why or why not, and then have a debate with your classmates to talk about reasons why helmet laws are a good idea or a bad idea.

To Learn More about Motorcycles

Beyer, Mark. *Motorcycles of the Past*. New York: Powerkids Press, 2002.

Davidson, Jean. *Growing Up Harley-Davidson*. Stillwater, MN: Voyageur Press, 2001.

Davidson, Jean. *Harley-Davidson Family Album*. Stillwater, MN: Voyageur Press, 2003.

Davidson, Willie G. *100 Years of Harley-Davidson*. New York: Bulfinch Press, 2002.

Gibbs, Lynne. *Mega Book of Motorcycles*. New York: Chrysalis Books, 2003.

Norman, Tony. *Motorbike Racing*. New York: Gareth Stevens Publishing, 2005.

Passaro, John. *The Story of Harley-Davidson*. Mankato, MN: Smart Apple Media, 2000.

Raby, Philip, and Simon Nix. *Motorbikes: The Need for Speed*. Minneapolis: LernerSports, 1999.

Rafferty, Tod. *Harley-Davidson: The Ultimate Machine*. Philadelphia: Courage Books, 2002.

Tiner, John Hudson. *Motorcycles*. Buffalo: Creative Education, 2003.

Wagner, Herbert. *At the Creation: Myth, Reality, and the Origin of the Harley-Davidson Motorcycle, 1901-1909*. Madison, WI: Wisconsin Historical Society Press, 2003.

Acknowledgments

I would like to thank my parents, Earl and Shirley Barnes, for their editing expertise and encouragement. Bobbie Malone, Sara Phillips, and the rest of the editorial staff at the Wisconsin Historical Society were also extremely helpful and easy to work with during the production of this book. The Harley-Davidson archives staff, including Maria DeWeerdt, Bill Jackson, and Dr. Martin Rosenblum, were instrumental in checking the book for accuracy and helping find suitable images. Historian Herbert Wagner provided essential historical information and advice. Finally, my wife, Amy, was unwavering in her love and support.

Index

This index points you to the pages where you can read about persons, places, and ideas. If you do not find the word you are looking for, try to think of another word that means about the same thing.

When you see a page number in **bold** it means there is a picture on that page.